Life and Non-Life in an Ecosystem

William B. Rice

Consultant

Leann Iacuone, M.A.T., NBCT, ATC
Riverside Unified School District

Publishing Credits

Rachelle Cracchiolo, M.S.Ed., *Publisher*
Conni Medina, M.A.Ed., *Managing Editor*
Diana Kenney, M.A.Ed., NBCT, *Content Director*
Dona Herweck Rice, *Series Developer*
Robin Erickson, *Multimedia Designer*
Timothy Bradley, *Illustrator*

Image Credits: pp.3-4, 9, 10, 12, 14-15, 17, 18, 20-24, 23, 24, 27, 31-32, Back cover iStock; p.5 NASA; pp.6, 25 Gary Hincks/Science Source; p.7 Richard Bizley/Science Source; pp.8 (background), p.11 Wally Eberhart/Getty Images; p.13 (top) Nigel Cattlin/Science Source, (bottom) David Scharf/Science Source; all other images from Shutterstock.

Library of Congress Cataloging-in-Publication Data

Rice, William B. (William Benjamin), 1961- author.
  Life and non-life in an ecosystem / William B. Rice
    pages cm
  Summary: "The ground you're standing on, the air you breathe, and the clouds you gaze at. They are all part of your home. They are also nonliving things. Living things don't only rely on one another; they also need nonliving things to survive. Everything in an ecosystem plays an important role."-- Provided by publisher.
  Audience: Grades 4 to 6
  Includes index.
  ISBN 978-1-4807-4716-6 (pbk.)
  1. Ecology--Juvenile literature.
  2. Biogeochemical cycles--Juvenile literature.
  3. Biotic communities--Juvenile literature. I. Title.
  QH541.14.R494 2016
  577--dc23
                                    2015002541

Teacher Created Materials

5301 Oceanus Drive
Huntington Beach, CA 92649-1030
http://www.tcmpub.com

ISBN 978-1-4807-4716-6

Table of Contents

Earth, Our Home

Sure, it's home. But what is it about this place called Earth that makes it as remarkable as we think it is?

Whether you live in a big city, a gentle rural countryside, or somewhere in between, you can see that there is a lot to life on Earth. Take a look at the birds and butterflies. Notice mountains and clouds, rocks and soils, smells and sounds. Notice the refreshing shade under a majestic tree. Notice the elegant smell of a rose on a sunny day and the vibrant smell of the air after it rains. Notice the unique sounds of cackling and cawing crows and the magical sound of a zipping hummingbird. Notice, too, the changing seasons throughout the year.

Life Out There

Many scientists believe that a planet must have plenty of carbon, water, and a few other elements for life to exist. Also, the planet must be the right size and distance from its star. However, we don't know for sure, as we have not found life anywhere else besides Earth.

Each of these things is noteworthy. But the importance of them is not in their beauty or usefulness. No, what makes them remarkable—what makes Earth remarkable—is the simple fact that on this planet, we have both life and non-life. And in all this vast universe, Earth is the only place *we know for sure* has this combination.

Now *that* is remarkable!

Searching for More

In 2003, NASA sent two robotic rovers to Mars. Their mission was to look around and send data back to Earth. Beginning in January 2014, the rovers began looking for any evidence of ancient life on Mars.

Developing Life

Earth wasn't always like this. Earth has undergone a lot of changes during its long existence. There was a time when Earth first formed that it was very hot and had a molten volcanic surface. There was no life.

However, over time, Earth cooled. Solid crust began forming. Liquid water began pooling. The atmosphere had very little oxygen and would not have been able to support creatures that are alive on Earth today. But over time, primitive organisms developed. They could live in these challenging conditions. These organisms began changing Earth little by little. They particularly began to change the atmosphere.

Here or There?

What we know about life comes from our studies of Earth. If life exists elsewhere in the universe, we might discover differences between life here and life there. Our definition of life may have to change.

This is what Earth may have looked like about 300 million years ago.

There are many ways this planet could have developed. But the story of how life evolved here includes all the right conditions somehow coming together. That's good news for every living thing on Earth!

What exactly makes something "living"? That is a complicated definition with many points of view. But most scientists agree on some basics. Living things…

- are complex and highly organized in their makeup.
- take in **energy** from their surroundings and use that energy.
- stay in **homeostasis**—balanced conditions internally that stay mainly the same.

- grow and develop.
- reproduce.
- respond to **stimuli**.
- evolve.
- have DNA or RNA.

In 1999, Scientists found bacteria that were 250 million years old.

Change Is Inevitable

Nonliving things can change **ecosystems**. Volcanoes are not alive, yet they can cause an environment to change completely. So can earthquakes!

Sometimes the differences between life and non-life can seem fuzzy. For example, there are nonliving things such as crystals that grow and respond to stimuli. But they are not alive. Entire books are written on just the definition of life! And every day, scientists make new discoveries. They understand life a little bit more.

No matter how we define it, we know that life developed on Earth through very particular conditions. What's more, life has affected the planet so that new life continues to evolve! For example, Earth's atmosphere today is what it is because of the life that has populated the planet over time. The atmosphere now is quite different from its earliest makeup. And life has affected Earth's geology. Some rocks are made of materials that were once part of living organisms!

Life and non-life in ecosystems affect each other in more ways than we know. Life depends on non-life for its existence. And non-life is changed by the existence of life. Because of this, planet Earth is an evolving system. If we could take a peek into the far distant future, who knows what we'd see!

In Between

Viruses are a topic of debate when it comes to life. Some say they are living because they grow, evolve, and have their own DNA or RNA. But viruses do not take in energy on their own, and they can't reproduce on their own, either. Do you think they are living or nonliving?

Ebola virus

Digging Deep

Even things as small as worms can affect nonliving things. They add air and water to soil. They also break down dead plants and turn them into matter plants can use. Worm poop is actually a fertilizer, which helps plants grow.

Large areas of plant life help to create an atmosphere that allows animals such as humans to live.

9

Soil

Soil is probably one of the most important things in an ecosystem. It is the loose dirt that is under our feet as we walk through a field or through a forest. Plants sink their roots deep into soil. Without soil, plants could not grow and live and animals would not have food.

People have been studying soils for centuries and have found that there are many different kinds of soils. Plants have adapted to growing in these different kinds. Soil is made up of several important parts. The parts include rock materials, pieces of dead plants and animals, liquids, air, and microorganisms.

Parent Soil

The small pieces of rocks and minerals that make up soil are formed out of parent material. Parent material is all of the larger rocks and minerals that become part of the soil.

Soils may take hundreds or thousands of years to form.

The best kind of soil for growing food is called *loam*. Loam is made of sand, silt, and clay. This combination of particles allows air and water to flow easily. The clay and silt hold in moisture. But the sand ensures that the plant doesn't receive too much water.

sand

loam

clay

Rock Materials

First, let's look at rock materials. Where do they come from? They are actually tiny pieces of rock that have broken off larger rocks and have been washed or carried down to lower areas by wind or water. These tiny pieces of rock are nonliving materials. Humans classify them mainly by their size. Clay is the smallest class of rock particles. Next largest is silt, and still larger are sand particles. Most soils have some particles from each of these groups. These particles provide soils with structure and support for the other soil parts. These particles also provide minerals and **nutrients** for plants and organisms to use for life and growth processes.

Decomposers

Soil is not only made up of tiny rock particles. It's also made up of small pieces of dead plants and animals. When a plant or animal dies, it falls to the ground. Plant parts such as dead leaves and branches also fall. They begin to decay and **decompose**, or fall apart. Decomposers, an important part of any ecosystem, actually break this matter down. Decomposers are mainly bugs and microorganisms. Soils are filled with these organisms. They include bacteria and fungi. Fungi are a common group of organisms that include yeast, molds, and **mycelia**. You've probably seen mold growing on cheese or bread that has been kept too long. And you probably know mycelia better by its fruit—mushrooms. Mycelia are underground organisms that form vast networks of **filaments** in soil. When the time is right, they grow mushrooms.

bleu cheese

Moldy Goodness

Even though mold is usually bad for you, some types of mold are used in things we eat! Mold is used to make certain types of cheese, such as bleu cheese. It is also used in antibiotics such as penicillin.

Microorganism is short for microscopic organism.

exposed mycelia network

bacteria in soil

Small but Important

Soil contains much more than meets the eye. It holds water and living organisms. You can find more microorganisms in a teaspoon of soil than there are people on Earth!

Instead of seeds, mushrooms have spores. Spores are released from mushrooms back to the ground. They begin to grow new filaments. They connect with other filaments to form new mycelia networks. As they do this, they break down rocks. They also decompose dead plants and animals and make nutrients available for plants to use. In addition, mycelia use minerals that come from the tiny rock pieces. They use energy and nutrients from dead plants and animals as well.

Water and Air

Water and air are also important nonliving parts of soil. Water is a special component that is used by just about every life form on Earth. Many scientists believe that water may be the most critical need of living things.

Water is needed by plants to grow and live. Plants use water for photosynthesis. They also use it to move nutrients within their plant bodies. Water occupies almost all of the space within plant cells. Water pressure in plants helps them stay upright. It also helps to orient their leaves to receive sunlight.

Within soil, water dissolves minerals and nutrients from rock particles. It also dissolves them from dead plant and animal materials. At the same time, these particles and materials provide structure and space for water.

vacuole

Plant Cells

All of the cells in a living thing have an important job to fulfill. In plant cells, there is a large vacuole that stores food and nutrients for plants. They also have a cell wall. Without the cell wall, the plant would collapse.

cell wall

100%

Nitrogen Cycle

One of the most important cycles on Earth, the nitrogen cycle, is a cycle in which nitrogen in the air and soil are turned into substances used by plants, which then return to the air and soil as plants decompose.

Extra nitrogen is released into the air.

Nitrogen falls in rain.

Waste and decay return nitrogen to the soil.

Bacteria fix nitrogen.

Plants take in fixed nitrogen.

15

Air is also found in soil. On average, soil contains 25 percent oxygen. Microorganisms living in soil require oxygen to live. Our bodies also need oxygen to work properly. We breathe in oxygen from the air around us. Oxygen taken in by our lungs allows our bodies to function properly. When we eat food, our cells produce energy. These cells are fueled by oxygen. Plants need carbon dioxide to work properly. Plants get carbon dioxide from the air in soil as well as the air above ground. The roots of plants not only take in water from the soil, but they also take in oxygen.

We breathe in oxygen and breathe out carbon dioxide. Plants breathe in carbon dioxide and breathe out oxygen. Carbon dioxide is also released from dead plant and animal tissues. Some of this carbon dioxide is found in soils and is used by plants. This exchange is a great partnership! It demonstrates very well the interdependencies of living and nonliving things.

Without plants, human beings would not have the oxygen they need to breathe.

Increasing CO$_2$

Carbon dioxide holds heat in the environment. Usually, this helps moderate temperatures. But in 2010, scientists found that soil and plants have been releasing more carbon dioxide than they have in the past.

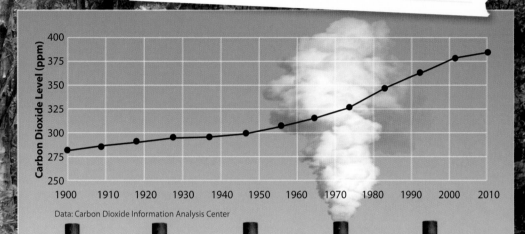

Data: Carbon Dioxide Information Analysis Center

About 50 percent of soil is air and water.

The Atmosphere

The atmosphere is the layer of air that surrounds Earth. It is also another key nonliving thing that affects all life in Earth's ecosystems. It is mainly made of nitrogen and oxygen. A small percentage is water vapor.

The processes that occur in Earth's atmosphere affect all types of ecosystems. As we know, an important part of Earth's atmosphere is oxygen. Animals need oxygen to live. We breathe it in without even thinking about it. Our bodies use this oxygen for many of our normal life processes. The atmosphere also has carbon dioxide. Plants need it just like we need oxygen. Plant cells use carbon dioxide to turn sunlight and water into food.

lightning

hail

hurricane

Fish breathe oxygen even though they live underwater.

Oxygen Cycle

The oxygen cycle is the movement of oxygen atoms from the atmosphere to animals and plants and finally to Earth's crust. Oxygen in Earth's crust is eventually released back to the atmosphere or taken up by plants and animals.

The most noticeable process in the atmosphere is weather. The atmosphere holds a lot of energy and heat. This energy and heat are spread unevenly. Because of this, there are winds and currents that carry the water vapor all over Earth. This makes storms of all sizes, from small storms to hurricanes. In each storm, water vapor falls to Earth as rain, snow, hail, or sleet. This brings water to ecosystems so plants and animals can use it.

Energy in the atmosphere also affects how warm or cold it is. In some ecosystems, such as the poles, it is cold most of the year. Ecosystems around the equator are mostly warm or hot all year. The ecosystems in between have periods of hotter and colder weather. These mainly depend on the seasons.

The usual type of weather in a place is its climate. Climate is based in part on the patterns of temperatures and **precipitation**. These patterns affect plants and animals. Certain kinds of each have adapted to live in different climates. Tropical climates are usually warm and rainy throughout the year. The plants and animals that live there need a lot of water and a pleasant temperature. The plants and animals that live in arid climates have evolved to thrive with little water and extreme heat and cold.

There are many different types of climates.

Mediterranean climate

Humans have become so numerous and active that we affect Earth's atmosphere and climate. We have used fossil fuels in many ways. This has released carbon dioxide and other gases at a faster rate than they can be used. These gases cause the atmosphere to keep more heat than it has in the past. The extra heat is beginning to cause changes in climate and weather. These changes include stronger storms, hotter temperatures, and extreme dryness or drought.

Average world temperatures have increased by around 1° Celsius (1.8° Fahrenheit) in the 20th century.

tropical climate

arid climate

This mountain peak in Colorado is an example of sunshine hitting one side of the mountain more than the other.

Location, Location, Location

An important condition for life in ecosystems includes orientation to the sun. Orientation is how a land feature is situated compared to the sun's rays. Here is an example: Imagine that a mountain has a north-facing and a south-facing slope. In North America, the south-facing slope gets more direct sunlight than the north-facing slope. Because of this, snow will stay on the north-facing slope longer than it does on the south-facing slope. More of the snowmelt also seeps into the soil on the south-facing slope. This is because it gets more sun, the snow melts sooner, and more water evaporates back into the atmosphere. One side gets and maintains much more water than the other side does. Because of this, there are different kinds of soils and different kinds of plants and animals on each slope, even though it's the same mountain. One slope has more water, and one has less; one has more sun, and one has less. The ecosystems on each slope are therefore quite different.

Adapting

Mountain goats have adapted to the various temperatures of mountain climates. Their thick coats protect them from the cold in winter. They shed these coats in the summer when it gets warmer.

Mountains, because they are so tall, intercept moisture in the atmosphere. There is more rain on one side of the mountain. The region that receives less rain is called the *rain shadow*. Death Valley, located in California, is a desert that is hot and dry because of a rain shadow. Succulents, cactuses, jackrabbits, and mountain lions reside here. On the other side of the mountain, there is much less water and more dry areas—even deserts.

At the equator, there is more direct sunlight than at Earth's North and South poles. This significantly affects the climate and weather patterns. The climate at the equator is hot and has rain. Here, camels, tarantulas, and antelope roam. The climate is much colder and has a lot less rain at the North and South poles. The Arctic fox, snowy owl, and reindeer live here. In between the tropics and poles, there are varying climates due to the seasons and wind patterns. In some places, there is more water than others. Some areas can be extremely dry deserts. Some areas can get very cold.

Elevation also plays a big role in the life and non-life found in ecosystems. Higher in the mountains, it is generally cooler with more precipitation. There is also less oxygen. The plants and animals have evolved and adapted to thrive in these conditions.

Death Valley

rain from expansion
and cooling

region of rain shadow

dry air

warm, moist air

evaporation from
warming

A Healthy Planet

Interdependence is key when studying both life and non-life on Earth. It is certain that life depends on non-life in order to live. Air, water, soil, and more are crucial to the ability to live and live well. And while non-life doesn't depend on life to exist, it is affected by living things.

But more than other living things, humans have the most ability to affect and alter the planet. It is an interesting irony that while we depend on Earth conditions to be exactly as they are in order to live, we can also be careless in how we treat the planet. We often take resources for granted and use more than we need. We easily forget that the conditions of our planet support us. We sometimes alter them without care or thought for the future.

Our home planet evolves all the time, as does life. Change is not a bad thing. But change that alters life processes can be harmful. It can harm not only Earth but ultimately the human race. In the interdependence equation, life and non-life must stay in balance. And that equals a healthy planet for every living thing.

Electric vehicles help reduce the carbon dioxide released into the atmosphere.

Think Like a Scientist

How do life and non-life affect each other? Experiment and find out!

What to Get

- 5–6 earthworms
- dark paper or cloth
- gardening gloves
- gardening soil
- large glass container with a lid, such as a bowl or an aquarium
- leaves
- sand
- water

What to Do

1 Moisten the soil and sand. Flatten the sand at the bottom of the container.

2 Flatten the soil above the sand. Place leaves on top of the soil.

3 Gently set the worms on top of the leaves and place the lid on the container. Be sure there are air holes.

4 Cover the sides of the container with dark paper or cloth so that it is dark inside the container. Each day, lift the paper or cloth to see inside. (Be sure to keep the sand and soil moistened so it doesn't dry out.) Make notes and take pictures of the changes you see each day. What do you notice?

Glossary

adapted—changed so that it is easier to live in a particular place

atmosphere—the mass of air that surrounds Earth

cells—basic units of life

decompose—to slowly break down and decay

ecosystems—communities of living and nonliving things in particular environments

energy—power that can be used to do something

filaments—thin, threadlike fibers

geology—the study of rocks and other substances that make up Earth's surface

homeostasis—a relatively stable state of equilibrium

microorganisms—tiny living things that can only been seen through a microscope

mycelia—the plant body of fungi, made of a mass of branching filaments that spread through soil

nutrients—substances that living things need to grow

organisms—living things

photosynthesis—the process in which plants use sunlight to combine water and carbon dioxide to make their own food (glucose)

precipitation—water that falls to the ground as rain, snow, sleet, or hail

stimuli—things that cause a change or a reaction

Index

YOUR TURN!

Water, Water Everywhere

Water is one of the most essential nonliving things that supports life. Take a notebook and jot down all the signs of water you see in a single day. Also note how living things use the water. What can you determine about water from what you see?